Juggling for the Complete Klutz

by John Cassidy and B.C. Rimbeaux
Illustrated by Diane Waller

KLUTZ®

KLUTZ

®creates activity books and other great stuff for kids ages 3 to 103. We began our corporate life in 1977 in a garage we shared with a Chevrolet Impala. Although we've outgrown that first office, Klutz galactic headquarters is still staffed entirely by real human beings. For those of you who collect mission statements, here's ours:

• Create wonderful things. • Be good. • Have fun.

Write Us
We would love to hear your comments regarding this
or any of our books. We have many!

KLUTZ®

557 Broadway
New York, NY 10012
thefolks@klutz.com

Distributed in the UK by Scholastic UK Ltd
Euston House, 24 Eversholt Street
London, NW1 1DB, United Kingdom

Distributed in Europe by Scholastic Ltd
Unit 89E, Lagan Road, Dublin Industrial Estate,
Glasnevin, Dublin 11, Ireland

Distributed in Australia by Scholastic Australia Ltd
PO Box 579, Gosford, NSW, Australia 2250

Distributed in Canada by Scholastic Canada Ltd
604 King Street West, Toronto, Ontario, Canada M5V 1E1

Distributed in Hong Kong by Scholastic Hong Kong Ltd
Suites 2001-2, Top Glory Tower, 262 Gloucester Road
Causeway Bay, Hong Kong

We make Klutz books using resources that have been approved according to the FSC™ standard which is managed by the Forest Stewardship Council™. This means the paper in this book comes from well managed FSC™-certified forests and other controlled sources.

ISBN 978-1-59174-448-1
8 8 8 0 7 5 8 5

MIX
Paper from
responsible sources
FSC™ C113204

This book is
dedicated to the closet
klutzes of the world...

Table of Contents

Foreword

Juggling for the Complete Klutz was first published as a mimeographed lesson plan in 1977 when I was a student teacher in Mountain View, California. Juggling was something I had learned at college and then refined a bit during summers spent guiding commercial river rafting trips. All of us guides were supposed to be at least marginally entertaining around the campfire, and my juggling act was definitely marginal.

After juggling had taken over my class, kicking out the English literature portion of the curriculum, I ran off another set of juggling instructions. As I fed the sheets into the copy machine I realized, with trembling hands and bated breath, that I was living the author's dream — my first book was going back to press.

A few weeks later, still reeling from the runaway bestseller success in my classroom, I began to dream of sudden fame and riches. The simple mimeographed lesson plan was enlarged and illustrated. Financing the printing of 3,000 copies of it (never mind the sewing of 9,000 bean bags) took some teamwork and I ended up talking two gullible classmates, B.C. Rimbeaux and Darrell Lorentzen, into sharing the risk of this grand venture.

We decided to call our partnership Klutz, Inc. We thought it was a suitably dignified name, given the extent of our ambition. We wanted to be in and out of business before the start of next summer's rafting season — hopefully with enough success to buy a small but lovely island in the Caribbean where we could settle down to a lifestyle of indulgence and excess. But we were realistic enough to understand that such an outcome wasn't guaranteed. We also had to consider the possibility of thunderous failure. We were prepared for that; in fact, we were basically planning on it.

The real outcome came as a terrifying shock. Instead of the sunny island of success, or the smoking crater of failure, we ended up with a low-rise of steady sales. Day in and day out, year in and year out, the orders kept coming in. It took quite a while for the full implication of this to completely penetrate. Klutz was a failed scam; Klutz was a career.

This was a large unpleasant pill to swallow for three just-out-of-college pals living very happily for most of the year in sleeping bags on various river banks. In fact, for the first few years, we subjected Klutz to some fairly aggressive neglect, half-hoping the whole thing would just go away. At one point, a 3-week drop in sales was traced to a 3-week failure to visit the post office box.

But circumstances conspired, marriage ensued, children were born and the career word began to lose some of its terror. In 1981, 4 years after *Juggling*, Klutz published its second book, on the game of footbag, and the slippery slope was slipped upon. Now, 30 years later, we have more than 150 titles in print and parents are beginning to buy Klutz books for their children because they remember them from their own childhood. This is a new and deeply disturbing development for those of us who have been here from the beginning.

Juggling, meanwhile, the little book that started it all, has been chugging along the whole while. Almost 3 million copies have been sold and we're down to only a handful of books that date from that first print run. For anyone who has ever run a hundred copies of their first book off a copy machine and dreamt great dreams for it — I offer this unlikely story as inspiration.

Over the years we have received thousands of letters from people who tell us their lives have been enriched, enlarged, enlivened and occasionally endangered by this little book and the skill it teaches. We treasure this knowledge and have come to believe the world is just a tiny bit sillier because of our efforts.

We couldn't be prouder.

So you're interested in learning how to juggle but it took you four years to learn how to tie your shoes and, besides, dropping things has always been second nature to you.

When your class picked teams, you were always picked last and then packed off to right field. Your mother always puts away the breakables whenever you step into the house. You're an original klutz and you probably think juggling is only for the super-coordinated.

Relax. Most people have got the moves down and are well on their way to juggling after only 15 minutes, and even hard-core cases like you won't be far behind.

It's **SIMPLE!** The motions are new and for the first couple of minutes they feel as awkward as brushing your teeth left-handed, but the truth is—they're easy, and anyone can do it.

As for the question of Why? I can only mumble vaguely about the unknowable nooks and crannies of the human spirit, or relate to you those times when I've found juggling to be just the answer for that slack moment or awkward minute. Perhaps you sometimes find yourself at a loss for a good "leave-'em-really-impressed" kind of parting line? At a job interview maybe, or on a first date, what could be more appropriate? My own experience suggests that hitchhiking may be the one arena where the juggler has a distinct advantage over his non-juggling competitor. Who could resist a little side-of-the-road razzle-dazzle?

Although the motions aren't difficult, they should be absorbed in bite-sized chunks. Otherwise, you'll run afoul of frustration, something that I will talk about a little later. In the meantime, read through the first three steps and glance at the pictures before picking up the bags. Don't bother reading about the problems just yet. They won't make sense until you have them, anyway.

STEP 1: THE DROP

Pick up all three bags and hold them briefly. You'll note that there is one more bag than you have hands, unless you are that rather rare case, in which event send away for our limited edition of *JUGGLING FOR THE EXCEPTIONALLY GIFTED.*

Throw all three bags into the air and, making no effort to catch any of them, let them all hit the ground. This is an example of **THE DROP.** I do it all the time and so will you, but it's good to familiarize yourself with the moves early on.

Practice **THE DROP** until the novelty wears off. Many people find this occurs quite rapidly, others seem to get a lot out of this exercise for quite some time. Leaving those folks to themselves, we'll move on.

STEP II: **THE TOSS**

Put two bags away for a time and hold just one, Cradle it in the center of your hand, not on your fingers. (Read that last line again. It's more important than you think.)

You should be standing relaxed, even grinning perhaps, your elbows near your body and your hands at about waist height. Toss the bag in easy arcs about as high as your eyes and as wide as your body, back and forth, hand to hand. It won't take you long to discover that this exercise is only a hair more interesting than the first, but you should keep at it a little longer. The important thing is to keep your tosses consistent, one after the other, so that you don't have to go lunging around catching weird throws.

Don't make your throws stiffly either. Use a natural "scooping" motion, as in the illustration. It's the most relaxed, natural way to toss. You're probably already doing it. Ideally, you should be able to "scoop" a toss up and have it land—eyes closed—in your other hand.

Realistically, if you can make the catch without having to dive for it, you'll be doing about normal.

Do this one until it gets boring. A minute seems to be about the limit for most people, but push yourself for a little more.

The "Scoop" Toss

STEP III: **THE EXCHANGE**

his is THE step, so pay attention. Read it all the way through before you do anything rash.

Pick up a second bag and cradle it in your hand so that you now have a bag in each hand. Look at the illustrations for an idea of what's going to happen here. I'll try to explain at the same time by hitting some of the key points and then going over some of the common problems—but don't let all the coaching throw you. Remember, it's a new motion so it's awkward at first, but persevere.

Using your best Step II toss, throw one bag up and over toward your other hand. Let it come to the top of its arc, and then, just as it starts to drop down into your other hand—which is holding the second bag—exchange the two, in one motion, by "scoop-tossing" the second and catching the first. Confusing, but look at the pictures and keep reading.

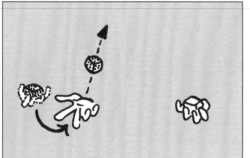

The First Toss
Your hand should move in a little scooping motion.

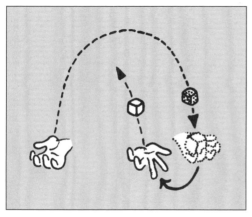

The Exchange
Your catching hand swings in to get rid of its bag and out to make the catch.

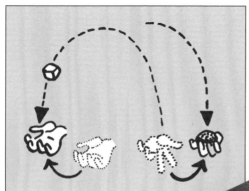

The Grand Finale
Catch in the one hand, catch in the other.

Juggling Truth #2:
All your tosses go UP
None go across.

Your second toss should pass to the inside of the first so that both throws **ARE IN THE SAME PLANE RIGHT THERE IN FRONT OF YOU.** Also, the path of the second toss should look the same as the first in terms of height and width. And remember, **THAT SECOND TOSS SHOULD NOT HAPPEN UNTIL THE FIRST HAS PASSED THROUGH THE TOP OF ITS ARC.** Otherwise, you will create all kinds of havoc. The exchange should be one smooth toss-and-catch motion.

All right, that's the way it's supposed to happen. Go ahead and work at it for a little bit and then come back and I'll talk about how it

Keep all the action in this frame (or at least try to).

really happened when you tried it. Incidentally, your first ten or so attempts are going to look and feel just terrible, so you might as well get used to that right away—but take heart, a mere ten minutes or so generally makes a big difference.

You're back, and you've got some problems. I know the feeling well, but read on. Help is on the way.

PROBLEM #1: The Panic Response

Your first throw goes OK, but the second is in total panic—impossible to catch. This is an obnoxious problem. The solution is ironclad mental control.

This is what is happening in your nervous system as you go through this routine: Your first throw goes up in a nice arc. Suddenly, your brain realizes that the hand that is going to have to make the catch *is already occupied!*

Your brain realizes there's only one reasonable thing to do: ***Panic!!***

A neural alarm flashes down to your occupied hand: "Collision emergency! Get rid of that other bag! Throw it anywhere, but ***CLEAR THAT LANDING SPACE!***"

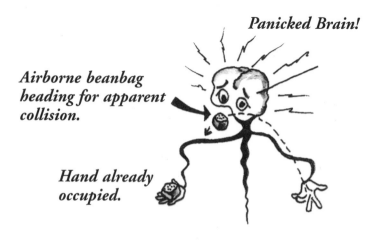

Panicked Brain!

Airborne beanbag heading for apparent collision.

Hand already occupied.

This is totally unnecessary. There's plenty of time to make a nice controlled scoop-toss, but your brain overreacts. Get a grip on yourself. Concentrate on your second toss. Swing your hand in, throw the bag up in a nice controlled arc just to the inside of the dropping bag, and then swing your hand back out to make the catch. You know you've done it perfectly when the second toss lands in your hand. No reaching. It all happens in a single plane (in other words, you should be able to do it right in front of a wall without banging your knuckles).

Some people respond differently to this problem of one bag heading for an already occupied hand. They have more control than that. Instead of panicking, they have . . .

PROBLEM #2: The Cheat Response

When these people see the first toss heading in for a landing on top of the second bag, it's no problem. They don't panic; they cheat. They clear the landing area by handing the problem bag back to the first hand; it never goes into the air. Then they think they've done something clever.

This Brain is CHEATING!

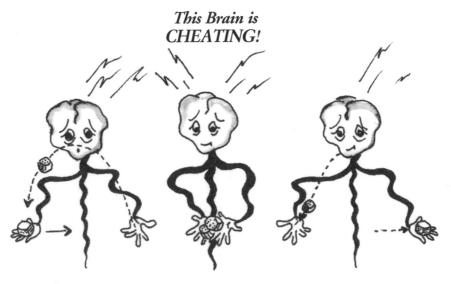

Brain sees oncoming collision.

Brain passes bag from hand to hand . . .

. . . and makes catch.

This is false! These people are deluding themselves.

Here is the Righteous Path:

The first bag goes up ...

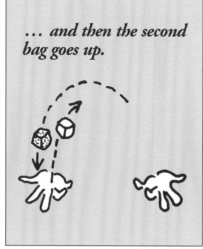

... and then the second bag goes up.

OK Enough words. Try your exchanges for 15 drops. Then take a break and try again for another 15. When you're starting to get the hang of it going one way (in other words, your first toss always comes out of one particular hand), switch. Start with your other hand. Give that one 15 drops and take another break. If everything still feels just terrible, take a look at STEP V: SPECIAL PROBLEMS.

Juggling Truth #3:
The second toss goes up
just like the first one did. It
does not go across. This is
the same truth as #2, but
that's how important it is.

STEP IV: **THE JUG**

 efore we start in on the final step, let me
describe how you're probably feeling.

You've put in some practice, you've paid some dues and you're starting to see some real progress. A bit of the awkwardness is gone, your tosses aren't as crazy, even your drops are becoming just a little less frequent. There's no other way to describe it—you're starting to feel the first faint glow of competence.

I'm joking, of course.

Actually, you've practiced forever and nothing good is happening. You're worse, in fact. Your tosses are still flying into the outfield and you're convinced juggling is every bit as hard as you thought it was.

But still, you're bone bored of the last step. If you're going to he a failure as a juggler, at least you're going to go down with three bean bags in your hands—not a lousy two.

I respect this kind of immaturity. Keep reading. The pictures on the facing page tell the whole story, but I want to make an important point first: I've lied to you. Step IV is not a new step. It's just Step III again, twice.

Why have I deceived you like this? Because basic juggling is only one step—The Exchange—the thing you've already been practicing. With three bags, you just have to keep doing them over and over in both hands. That's all. It's a chain, and you've been working on a single link. Now you're going to put two of them together.

Deep Breath

The First Toss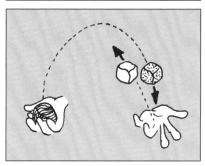

The First Exchange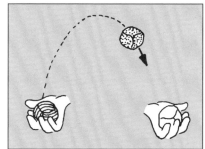

The Second Exchange

Note that your hands weave back and forth ("scoop tossing") so that the upgoing bag can avoid the downgoing one.

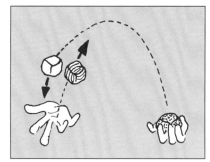

If you can do this much, I'm amazed—take a low bow. You're JUGGLING!!! All this time you thought juggling was keeping two or three things in the air at once. Now you should be able to see that there's really only one thing flying around—the others are just being held until they get exchanged with the flier, one at a time.

If you can put two exchanges back to back, I call that a "jug." Two jugs would be four exchanges in a row without a drop.

Once you can do a jug there'll be no stopping you. But let me explain what will undoubtedly start happening. In the heat of the moment you'll forget to concentrate on your tosses and they'll begin to fly out away from you, resulting in the "sprinting juggler syndrome."

When this starts to happen (and don't worry, it happens to everyone), remember what you learned about keeping your exchanges in one plane by tossing each bag to the *inside* of the dropping bag's arc. And don't start using your whole arm to make your tosses, either. Keep your elbows pretty close to your sides and your hands at about waist height. Practice in front of a wall if you want, but . . .
CONCENTRATE ON WHERE YOU'RE PUTTING THOSE TOSSES!

To continue in this vein is to run the risk of becoming a nag. And so I will leave you with no more warning than this: Take frequent breaks while you're trying to learn. Twenty minutes spent in two ten-minute spurts is much more effective than in one lump.

And when all else fails, remember these few words of wisdom that have guided me through more than just a few trying times: "It's always darkest just before it gets pitch black."

STEP V:
SPECIAL PROBLEMS

Almost everyone seems to have a strong tendency to turn to this section too soon. Deep in our hearts we all figure we're exceptional—one way or another—and consequently deserving of some special attention.

It is often a deeply humbling experience to realize that our problems are neither very unusual, nor even very serious. So I will try to break this to you as gently as I can. If you've been trying for ten minutes or so and are still dropping a lot or having trouble keeping all the action right there in front of you (here it comes, so steel yourself), you're probably doing quite well—just suffering from a mild shortage of practice. Try it for a little longer and then take a break. You'll get less frustrated that way and it will give your muscles a chance to think about it all.

After a little while, pick up the bags and try it again with renewed concentration. If it still doesn't click at all, read on and see if you can recognize whatever it is that's holding you up.

PROBLEM: You're on STEP III: THE EXCHANGE, with just two bags, but you can't seem to make it work. You flub up the toss, you flub up the catch . . . everything feels terrible, and you've tried and tried.

In two-person juggling, your brain doesn't have to think as hard.

BEST SOLUTION: Go get yourself a friend—you probably need one about now anyhow—and have her stand next to you, shoulder to shoulder. You can hold hands if you want, or if you're not that kind of friends, you can each put your inside hand behind your own back. With your outside hands you're going to be doing exchanges. This is how it goes:

Both players start with one bag in their hands.

Step One: She tosses a bag up and over to the target (your hand).

Step Two: You wait until her toss has peaked out, then you toss your bag back and catch hers.

Your throw should go just inside her incoming bag. Doing exchanges like this (with two people) should slow things down enough so that you can eliminate the element of panic from your tosses. Change places with your friend after a little while so that you can loosen up both hands.

If you and your friend happen to be a particularly smooth team, you might want to extend this exercise into something that might be called "Siamese-twin" juggling. All you have to do is add a third bag to the act, which quickens things up a bit, but not too badly. Instead of doing one exchange and stopping, you're going to be doing a bunch of exchanges back-to-back (or, I should say side-to-side).

If you can get some kind of relaxed and confident expression on your faces while you're doing this, then you've got your first trick—which isn't bad progress at all.

SECOND BEST SOLUTION: Since this is really just a psychological problem, there are a couple of possible psychological solutions.

One that I have used with some success is the idea of throwing the second bag through an imaginary wire loop "attached" to the dropping bag.

Try this for one or two exchanges. At the finish of each exchange, stop and ask yourself if your throw went through the loop. If it didn't, ask yourself how much you missed by. If you can tell yourself how far off you were, then you've got your concentration focused on the right place, i.e., the placement of that second toss.

Another use of the same idea is to paint little targets on the palms of your hands. This can make for awkward explanations during the non-juggling portion of your day, though, and I offer it only as a suggestion.

The bag going up and the bag going down pass very closely. A near-collision is perfect

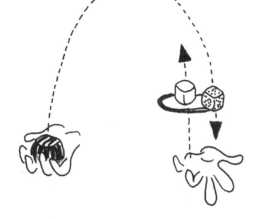

PROBLEM: You're on STEP IV: THE JUG, and you are a serious sprinting juggler. There is no way you can keep your throws under control.

SOLUTION: First of all, practice in front of a wall so that you can't throw them too far out in front of you. An alternative is to try it sitting down. (I've never found this to be so great, but everyone else says it helps, so I'll pass it on.) As a last resort, you might try practicing on the edge of a cliff. A close friend of mine (rest his soul) used to swear by this one.

PROBLEM: Your legs are killing you from picking up your drops all the time.

SOLUTION: Stand over a table, hire a bag boy, OR BUILD YOUR OWN RETRIEVAL SKIRT (see illustration above for construction details).

Beyond the Basics

nce you've smoothed out your three-bag juggling and can do it without having to dash across the room, you'll probably start wondering about the next step. Your friends, too, will be getting bored with your new little act. "What about four?" they'll ask innocently. Or even better, "How many can you do?" as if anything less than 11 would put them to sleep.

Juggling is not a spectator sport! If you want to be rid of these ingrates who don't know real talent when they see it, your only recourse is to stop juggling, hand them some bags and show them how to do The Toss. They'll be hooked in no time. And once they are, you've got partners for team juggling, which probably ought to be your first trick on your way to Ringling Brothers.

STEALING: You and your partner both ought to be at least fairly decent jugglers before you try this one. By that I mean you should each be able to do 20 or more jugs without dropping.

Ingredients: two people and three juggling bags.

Let your partner begin this one. As he juggles merrily away, stand right beside him shoulder-to-shoulder, at the ready. For the first few attempts, this by itself will make him nervous enough to drop everything in hysterics. Once you've matured your way over that little hurdle, you can go on.

What you are going to do here is interrupt his juggling by taking two **SUCCESSIVE** throws—one right after the other—just as they reach the tops of their arcs. That should leave you holding two bags. If your partner is cooperating, he can direct that third bag over your way. As it starts to drop into one of your (occupied) hands, just do an exchange, and you're off on your own, juggling away.

VICTIM   THIEF

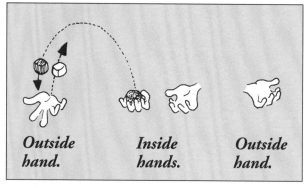

Outside hand.   **Inside hands.**   **Outside hand.**

First steal.

With his outside hand, thief takes a throw from victim's outside hand.

VICTIM   THIEF

Thief steals very next throw.

Second steal.

Victim cooperates and tosses last bag over to thief.

Victim tosses last bag.

Victim left empty-handed.   Thief juggles away.

PASSING: This is the basic act in team juggling and it requires two pretty smooth jugglers. In other words, each of you ought to be able to do 30 or more jugs without a drop and still maintain calm.

Ingredients: two of the aforementioned type of jugglers, and six bean bags.

Arrange yourselves so that you're facing each other a few feet apart. In your right hands put two bags, in your lefts, one. Each of you start juggling, but make an effort to start together and stay in time—in other words, synchronously. It helps a lot if one of you counts out loud every time a toss leaves your right hand, "1 . . . 2 . . . 3."

OK. On a prearranged number, say three, instead of tossing across to your *own* left hand, throw your bag in a nice, easy arc over to your *friend's* left hand. And, at the same time, she should be doing exactly the same thing.

If it works out (and it won't for a while), both of you will juggle along, switch two bags, and continue juggling—all without really missing a beat.

Juggling along.

If you were able to do it, this is how it would look:

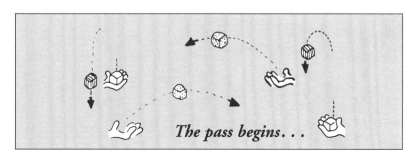

The pass begins . . .

. . . and finishes.

And back to . . .

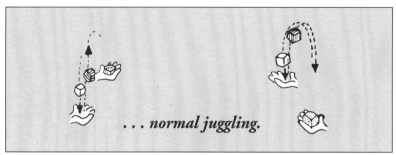

. . . normal juggling.

Passing sounds tricky because it is, but there are a few warm-up exercises that can help.

While you're holding a bag in each hand, have your friend toss you a third—into your left hand. Before it lands, do an exchange and begin your own juggling. After a few moments juggling on your own, throw her one back—from your right hand—and stop.

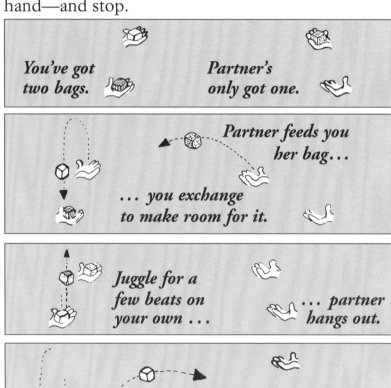

You've got two bags.

Partner's only got one.

Partner feeds you her bag...

... you exchange to make room for it.

Juggle for a few beats on your own ...

... partner hangs out.

You toss back...

...partner catches.

Start by holding three bags and giving your friend a fourth. Begin juggling (and counting) and then, on "three," make the toss over to your friend who—at the same time—should feed your hand with a nice easy toss. Your friend won't be juggling during this exercise. Her job is strictly to catch your one toss while feeding you another. If it's done smoothly, you can juggle along without missing a beat.

You're juggling along.

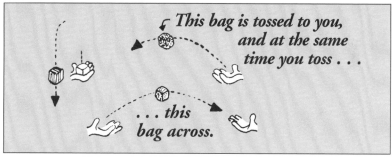

This bag is tossed to you, and at the same time you toss . . .

. . . this bag across.

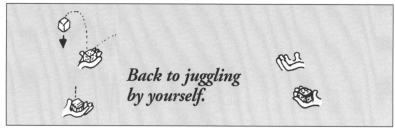

Back to juggling by yourself.

Switch back and forth on all these exercises so that both of you can get it at the same time.

When you're by yourself, you can practice passing by standing in front of a wall and bouncing every third toss out of your right hand off the wall and into your left.

Just so you don't feel unusually handicapped, I'll describe the major problem that seems to get everyone when they try passing for the first time.

EVERYBODY'S PROBLEM: You'll be juggling along, both of you in time. On the third throw out of your right hand, you'll do it just the way you're supposed to. Both your right-hand tosses will go across, you'll catch them, and then . . . chaos. The whole thing will fall apart because you'll try to throw the next one over there, too. Meanwhile, your partner's going through the same thing. Mass confusion.

It's another psychological problem. You're in the habit of keeping all your tosses to yourself. You break it for one toss over to your partner, and then . . . you can't get back into the old rut, and you panic.

As usual, the cure is practice. If you're not too proud to go backwards, Warm-up Exercise #2, described on page 33, is the least painful way to get it.

There will come a time, perhaps even in your lifetime, when you'll be able to execute this passing trick with a certain amount of flair, even repeatedly.

This, then, is the time for graduation ceremonies. Instead of just tossing across to your partner on every third throw, toss *every* right-hand bag across— while she does the same. Magnificent.

There are variations on this, of course. While you're both juggling, you can each whistle the same tune or a different tune. She can talk. You can talk. You can memorize poems.

Abbott and Costello had a two-part routine called "Who's on First?" It takes about ten minutes. If you and your partner are able to recite this routine while team juggling, send me your address. I will fly there immediately.

Circle Juggling

My own first, misguided attempts at juggling took this circular form where the objects follow one another around in one direction. Back in those days I never could get it, but a great deal of fruit and occasionally eggs went down in the effort.

Probably the most frustrating part of circle juggling is the fact that it is harder to learn than normal-style juggling—you have to keep *two* things in the air at once, but it looks as if there's only one. In regular juggling, the exact opposite is the case.

Anyway, so much for the editorial. The diagrams should give you a pretty good picture of how to do it. You'll start with two bags in your "best" hand—be it right or left—then toss them both up in quick succession in identical arcs heading over to your other hand. As soon as you've cleared your good hand, you'll have to cross the third bag into it in a quick, underneath throw.

Then all you have to do is keep everything going around in a circle. Good luck.

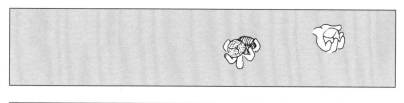

Two quick identical throws...

...clear the hand that's going to make the catch in a quick cross-over toss.

Overhand Grabbing

This is just another way to make your catches. Instead of passively letting a bag land in your hand, reach up and grab it with an overhand motion. Then resume your normal juggling routine.

Bag is caught in a downward snatch.

When you can do this consistently with either hand, you can try to toss from that overhand position (a more difficult venture). To make the toss after you have grabbed a bag, don't turn your hand back over—keep your palm down. Then flick your wrist upward, releasing the bag. This will leave your hand in a position to grab that next bag. If you can do this with every toss, you'll not only be fairly good, but you'll also have the appearance of practicing the high-speed dog paddle, which is pretty strange behavior. But by this time your friends should be used to anything.

Outside Juggling

This is clearly a case where a diagram is worth far more than all of my wordiness. Just look at the picture and concentrate on keeping all your tosses soft.

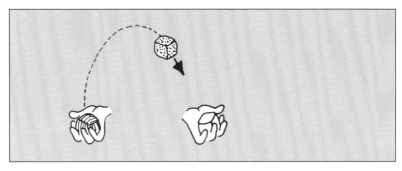

This bag goes up on the outside of the other, down-going bag. Tricky.

Ditto with the other hand.

The "Blind" Juggler

This is an interesting trick, but I include it with some reluctance because it requires one very quick-handed juggler, and since quick-handedness and klutziness are not often associated, this might create a problem.

Nevertheless, it's such a different kind of trick that I couldn't resist.

Stand face-to-face with your partner about two or three feet away. One of you is going to have to be the quick-handed one while the other can be a seriously klutzy type. Settle it among yourselves as to who's who. The rest of my comments, though, will be directed to she of the quick hands.

The klutz will be the "blind" juggler, so he should close his eyes and then begin to juggle, just as if his eyes were open. But as the first bag leaves his hand,  your job is to intercept it at the top of its arc and then manually (and quickly!) place it in his other hand just as he's releasing his second bag. You'll catch that one with your other hand and repeat the "manual exchange" in your *partner's* other hand.

The whole picture should look like this: Your partner—eyes closed—will be juggling, but you'll be catching his every throw and putting them in his hands, right in beat with a normal juggling pattern.

The big problem is staying up with your partner and also getting your hands out of the way as his throws come up. Not easy, I admit, but still an interesting trick.

Razzle Dazzle

This is the category of pure flash. Things like making one toss from behind your back or under your leg. Or catching your final bag by stooping over and letting it land on the back of your neck. Another one consists of popping a bag up with your knee or foot rather than doing a normal exchange.

Specific directions for all these would read like an anatomy textbook and, besides, they probably wouldn't be very helpful anyway.

My only hint, if you are looking to put a little of this kind of flash in your routine, is to always heave one bag especially high before you go into whatever contortions you have in mind You can buy yourself some needed extra time with the additional height.

Two-in-one Pattern

This is an entirely different way to keep three objects juggled and requires that you learn how to keep two things in the air with only one hand.

It takes some time before you can do this with any kind of consistency, so you should concentrate on learning it in the hand that you're best with. If it seems a lot harder than normal juggling, that's because it is.

At least while you're learning, you should always keep your throws going to the inside of the bag that's dropping down. This creates a kind of circular pattern. Check the diagram carefully. Unfortunately, there aren't any secrets to learning this technique—just spread it out so you don't feel overly frustrated at any one time.

Round and . . .

. . . around.

Air traffic control is the biggest problem—avoiding collisions and not panicking.

After you feel relatively comfortable keeping two objects juggled like this, then you can bring the third bag and your other hand into the act by just tossing it up and down in time.

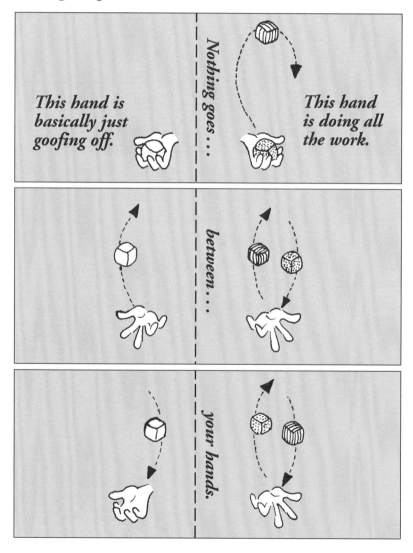

This hand is basically just goofing off.

Nothing goes . . .

This hand is doing all the work.

between . . .

your hands.

Note: You can fake this pattern by keeping hold—and never letting go—of the third bag. Then lift it and bring it down in time. A great trick because audiences love it way out of proportion to how hard it is.

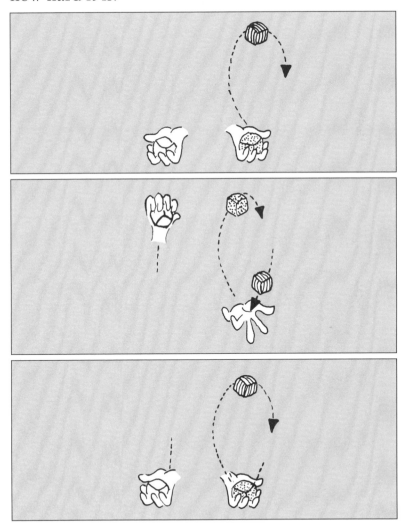

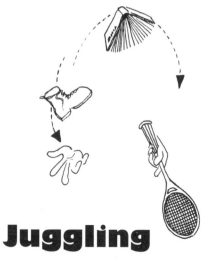

Juggling
with Various Objects

This has always been my strongest suit, and I consider myself a near-expert on the kinds of things that can be juggled.

First of all, the obvious: balls. My main hesitation about balls is that they are fine enough for juggling, but very bad for dropping. And since dropping is always a big part of my act, I have trouble with balls rolling under the furniture, dropping down storm drains, etc. Jugglers who don't incorporate dropping into their act as much as I do often favor hard rubber lacrosse balls; they're expensive, but they are great for tricks where you have to bounce them off the floor rather than simply toss them between your hands.

The diagram should give you a good idea of what's supposed to happen.

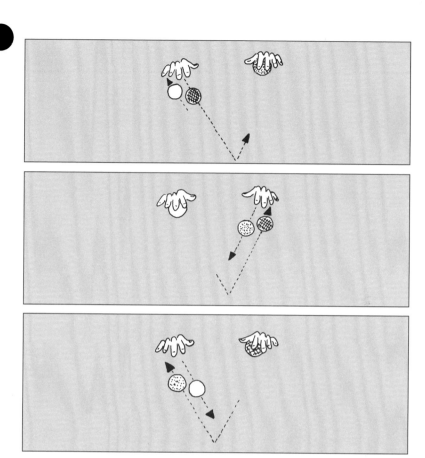

CAUTION: if you live in a second-story apartment, you probably ought to skip this one.

Edibles

For a beginning juggler, the produce department of any grocery store can take on a wonderful new dimension. My own favorites are the bananas. They're difficult to get the hang of at first, but even a little practice pays off quickly. If you don't try to flip them end for end, you'll find it easier.

After bananas, of course, come apples, oranges, pears (when they're in season), even cantaloupes— although the weight here can be a problem.

Grapes are especially good because you can wrap up your little act by throwing them all high in the air and then catching them in your mouth. Depending on age group and interests, this can be very impressive to the person you're shopping with.

I now have a special bonus for all of you who are still here reading this book, slogging away. Because here, buried in the underbrush on this page, is the best trick in the book, by far. It's quite simple, and yet it never fails to get a huge response. In other words, it's the perfect Klutz trick. It's the Amazing Eat-the-Apple Trick:

Step One: Keep a careful eye out for grocery clerks.

Step Two: Take three apples and begin juggling them normally. It helps if one of them is green and the other two are red.

Step Three: When the green one gets to your right hand, make a special effort to throw it high in the air—say about three or four feet. Keep it within reason, though, or you'll be visible from the next aisle.

Step Four: With the extra time you've got, bring the left-hand apple up and grab a bite out of it. If you're quick enough, you can get your hand (with bitten apple) back in place in time for the high flier to land there. You'll do an exchange and then continue juggling.

As I say, *very* impressive.

CAUTION: This can be a pretty messy trick, so you probably ought to dress accordingly. Also, if you don't want to eat the stem, you should twist it off at the beginning since you'll be too busy once you get started.

The Need to Juggle with Eggs

Personally, I love juggling with eggs. And, as a result, I have mopped many a kitchen floor. But once you've tasted the adrenaline of seeing all that fragile young poultry flying above your hands, it's impossible to stop.

The Section on Clubs

Juggling clubs are those things that look like bowling pins. For most people who've managed to achieve a state of bean bag competency, clubs are the next place to go. At the juggler's conventions these days, clubs outnumber balls or bean bags ten to one. The reason for their popularity is simple: Team juggling is more fun than solo juggling, and club passing is the best kind of team juggling.

Performing jugglers have always tended to favor clubs because all that flying lumber looks so impressive, not to mention visible from the back of the hall.

Fortunately for the rest of us, they're not nearly as tricky as they seem. In fact, once you're past the original "What-in-the-world-do-I-do-with-these-things" hump, you'll find they're actually harder to drop than bean bags.

Where to Get Juggling Clubs

You can make very classy clubs by shortening the handles (use a saw) of three rubber suction plumber's helpers. Don't laugh. It works pretty well, but if you want to buy clubs specifically designed for juggling, go shopping online.

STEP 1: THE FLIP

This is it. The basic move in club juggling. You have to burn it into your alpha-wave subconscious neuropatterns. (They're the ones you see when you squeeze your eyes really tight.)

Start with one club held like the diagram shows. Flip it over to your other hand—it should peak just a little over your head—and catch it around the neck. Don't clonk yourself. You know you've done it right when you don't have to move your catching hand. The club just lands in it.

Ten minutes later. . .

Boring, isn't it? Pick up the second club and add some challenge.

The chances that you will be able to do this properly on the first try are zero ...

... however, flipping and catching a club is only a little harder than tossing and catching a bean bag.

3.

2.

1.

Doing an exchange with two clubs requires two good, relaxed accurate flips. Just as the first flip peaks out and starts down, toss the other one just to the inside of the dropping club (identical pattern to bean bag juggling).

You'll probably go through some of the same panic responses that you first went through with bean bags. The desperate catches, the weird throws . . . familiar ground by now. The only new variable in the flip is the speed at which you turn the club. When you've turned it too quickly or too slowly, catching it around the neck becomes a true challenge.

Practice, practice, practice. . .

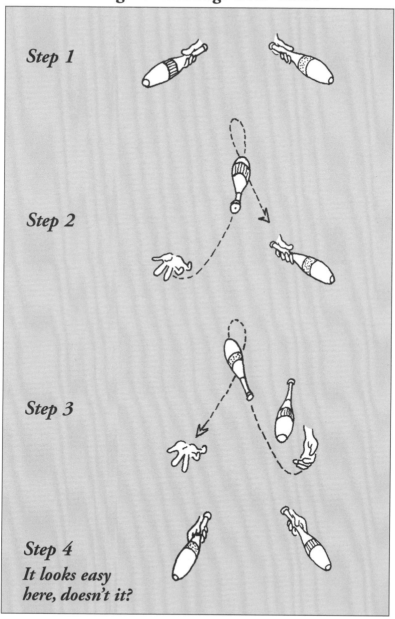

Step 1

Step 2

Step 3

Step 4
It looks easy here, doesn't it?

Once you can manage two clubs, of course, three becomes an irresistible goal. Getting started with three seems a bit awkward at first because putting two clubs in one hand seems such a squeeze. Check the diagram for the right grip.

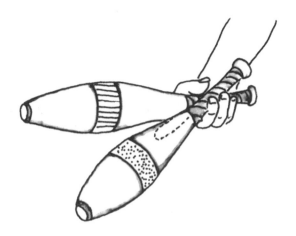

Start with the hand that has two things in it, just like you did with three bean bags. Count out loud as you toss each club and when (and if) you get to three, stop. That's a jug. You're on your way to the circus.

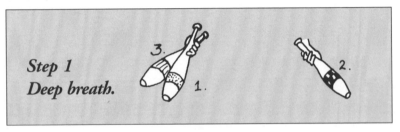

Step 1
Deep breath.

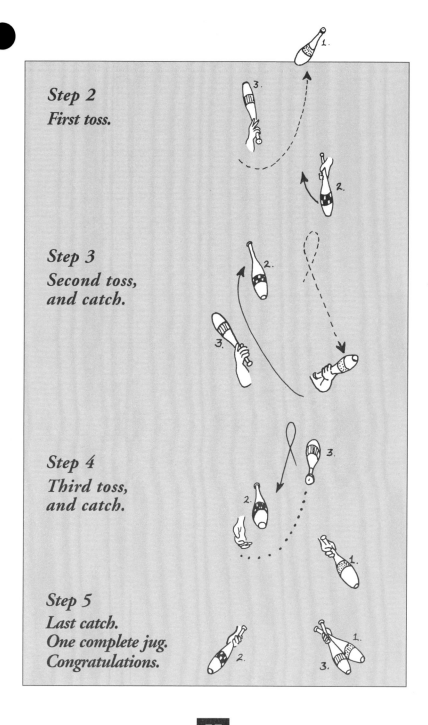

Step 2
First toss.

Step 3
Second toss,
and catch.

Step 4
Third toss,
and catch.

Step 5
Last catch.
One complete jug.
Congratulations.

Club Passing

Although you may have your doubts at first, there will come a time when you can juggle with three clubs with reasonable ease. At that point, you should start looking for a partner, because team juggling is the name of the game. Passing clubs with a partner (or partners) is a lot of fun. There's no way around it.

The steps to learning the basic club pass are identical to those outlined for bean bag passing (page 30). You'll need six clubs, two people and a clear space to work in. Start with just three of the clubs and two people. Spread yourselves out about 12 feet and warm yourselves up with the following exercise:

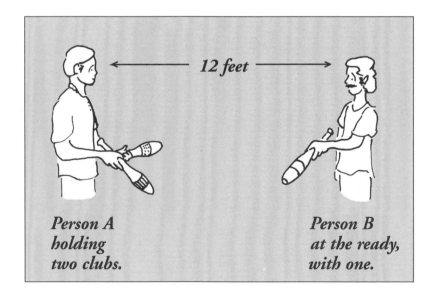

Person A holding two clubs.

Person B at the ready, with one.

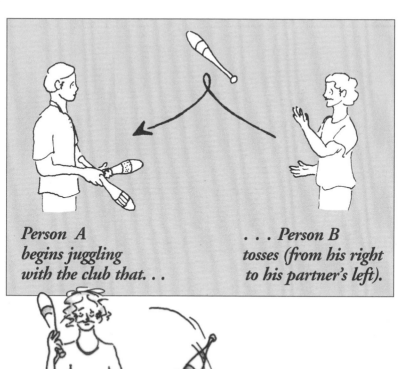

Person A
begins juggling
with the club that. . .

. . . Person B
tosses (from his right
to his partner's left).

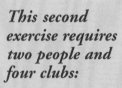

*This second
exercise requires
two people and
four clubs:*

*Person A
juggling merrily away.*

*Person B
poised.*

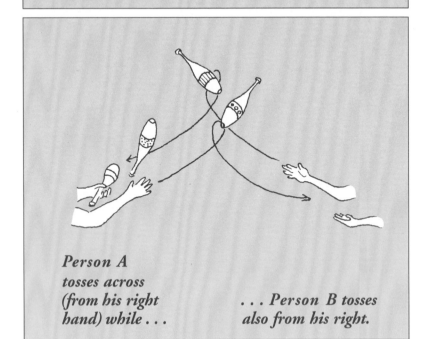

*Person A
tosses across
(from his right
hand) while . . .*

*. . . Person B tosses
also from his right.*

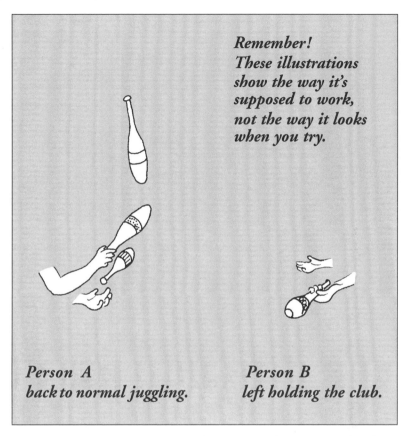

Remember!
These illustrations
show the way it's
supposed to work,
not the way it looks
when you try.

Person A
back to normal juggling.

Person B
left holding the club.

Once you can manage this second exercise fairly well, you're on the brink of success. Now each of you should pick up your last club. Both of you should be standing there, each nervously clutching three clubs.

Start juggling in sync. The best way to do this (all the pros do it this way) is to lift your clubs chest high. Your partner does the same, then on a signal, both of you bring them down and start juggling.

Count every time a club leaves your right hand: 1 . . . 2 . . . 3, flip to your partner's right hand while he does the same. Continue juggling, counting and tossing on every third right-hand throw. Bring in an audience.

Step 1.   Juggle in sync. Count on every right-hand toss.

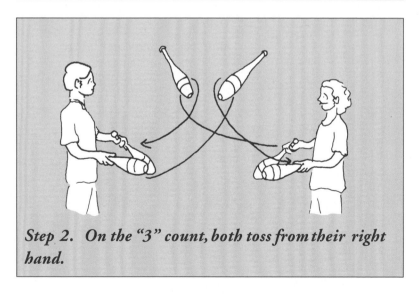

Step 2.   On the "3" count, both toss from their right hand.

Step 3. (Ideal) Both catch the passes and go back to self-juggling.

Step 4. (Reality) No one catches anything. One club hits shoulder. Another bounces off chin.

Higher Math in Club Passing

Let's say you've defied everyone's predictions and actually learned how to do this trick. Now you are into the world of serious craziness. Jugglers hold conventions where crowds of them pass clubs back and forth like a choreographed pie fight. If you can juggle between two people, adding any additional number of people just changes the direction you're tossing to and catching from. The pattern and individual moves are identical. All you'll need is split vision.

As long as you're into these advanced realms, you can experiment with the timing of your pattern. Don't limit yourselves to every third throw. Flip every other right-hand throw, or *every* right-hand throw . . . or you can try the ultimate . . .

Random Passing

Two of you juggle along—then, whenever the urge strikes, toss across without the slightest warning. Your partner now has about one panic-stricken second to do the same before she has to catch yours and continue juggling. Extremely tricky.

There's no limit to where you can take club passing. For most jugglers, this is where they spend the rest of their juggling lives. It combines the camaraderie of team sports with the solo skills of juggling. From here, it goes on forever. You can contact the International Jugglers' Association (P.O. Box 7307, Austin, TX 78713-7307) if you'd like to attend a convention and get into one of the pie fights. They're great fun and don't worry, jugglers of every skill level attend.

Tricks with Clubs

Let your imagination roam. Anything you can do with bean bags you can do with clubs. Behind the back. Between the legs. All that stuff.

You can toss them without the flip ("floaters") for a little extra challenge. Or you can double- or triple-flip them ("spinners").

One trick unique to clubs is the "kick-up." *Very* impressive—but it'll be at least a couple of days before you'll even begin to get the hang of it. The idea is to pick up a dropped club with your foot and flip it back up into a juggling pattern. (No more humiliation as you bend over to pick up drops.)

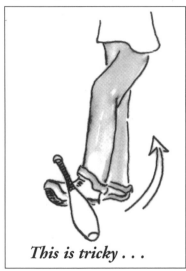

This is tricky . . .

. . .but not impossible.

The Kick-up

For the kick-up, you have to rest the neck of the club over the top of your foot. Lifting the club from this position may seem impossible, but the trick is to catch the knob on your shin as you swing your foot out and up (not unlike the dog-sees-hydrant move). Properly done, the club will come up with a single flip.

Juggling Various Strange Club-like Objects

After you've mastered the basic club flip, a whole new category of weird things becomes juggleable: flying hatchets, torches, small chainsaws, flaming knives . . . that sort of thing.

Personally, I tend to shy away from sharp things that are on fire. I do have a specialty though—rubber chickens. And plumber's helpers (those big rubber suction things). I have a "rubber-chicken-plumber's-helper-and-egg routine" that is just about ready for prime time.

Numbers Juggling

T his is the section where I'm finally going to talk about juggling with more than three objects. I've deliberately saved it for the end because it's a special case, with mental health implications.

At this point, you are probably juggling three objects (clubs, bean bags, chinaware, rubber chickens . . .) with casual flair. You feel a certain sense of pride and accomplishment. Your friends, though, are bored. They want four.

Learning how to juggle with four objects is not all that tricky. I'll go over the steps here in a minute, but before you start in on it, you should recognize that four is not what your friends *really* want. What they really want is one more than whatever you can do. This is the infamous Numbers Game Trap.

On a scale of 1 to 10, learning how to juggle with three objects is a 2. Learning how to juggle with four objects is a 5. Learning how to juggle with five, figure 34. Beyond that I can't count that high. Enrico Rastelli, an Italian juggler who was active 70 years ago, is considered history's finest juggler. He reportedly could juggle 11 objects. He also practiced 12 hours a day.

There are a zillion tricks and variations with three objects and passing patterns. More than enough to occupy a lifetime.

Having said all that, I know that there are those of you out there who must know how it is done. It is for their doomed sake that I set these instructions down.

Four-object Juggling

In order to juggle with four, you will have to develop your "off" hand in the same way that you developed your "good" hand for the "two-in-one" patterns. If you're right-handed, that means you'll be working with your left—and vice versa.

Clearly this is going to take some time. Your object is to keep two bean bags juggled with only one hand (your "off" hand) and do it under control.

If you can get over that hurdle, then you'll have reached the point of no return, so I might as well play the rest of this out.

A. Put two bags in each hand. Practice for a moment keeping the two in your right hand going.

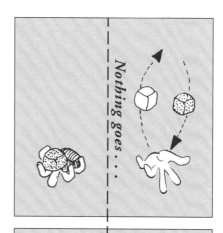

B. Then stop and practice uith your left.

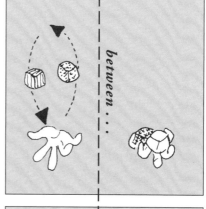

C. Then (deep breath) practice with both hands simultaneously. You do not cross any bags between hands.

Note: *Don't start with both hands simultaneously. Stagger your starts— one . . . two.*

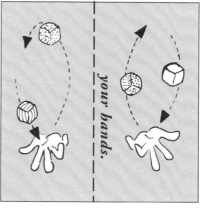

Five-object Juggling

The black belt of juggling. I have never heard of anyone learning how to juggle five objects with less than three months' effort. If that doesn't scare you off, nothing will.

Put three bags in one hand, two in the other, and stand over a big bed. Starting with your three-bag hand, toss one up in a high, perfectly accurate arc over to your other hand. But before it even peaks out, toss one out of your other hand in another perfectly accurate arc. And then (are you still there?) toss the second bag out of your first hand.

So, if we freeze the action for a second here, this is what it looks like. There are three things in the air—all perfectly thrown on arcs that pass one another, but are nevertheless identical in terms of height and width. Their arrangement over your hands should be as illustrated. Two bags are still being held.

Now, as each flying bag drops into your hand, you'll change it with the flier—and in this way (theoretically)

you should be able to keep everything going.

The pattern used in juggling five things is identical to the pattern used in juggling three, but I can't emphasize enough the difference between having three things in the air and having one.

The difficulty, as will soon become apparent, is that each and every toss has to peak out at exactly the same height. Otherwise, the pattern will disintegrate. For a good long time (like, months), this will not seem even remotely possible.

There are a couple of things that might help in training. At first, don't make any effort at catching. Throw all five bean bags up, in as good a pattern as you can, and then watch and listen as they hit the bed. The three that left your right hand should fall into a tight cluster directly underneath your left hand, and the two that left your left hand should do the same under your right hand. (They won't, of course, but they should.) You should also be able to hear five distinct "plops" indicating that all five bags kept their original spacing. An alternative to a big bed is a partner engaged in the same five-object quest. The two of you should stand face-to-face, a foot or so apart. Let's say you're the one holding the bags. Throw them all up in your best pattern and then forget about them. Your partner should try to catch them all. If your tosses were reasonably accurate, this is not impossible. Then reverse the process. Back and forth. (Credit to Dave Finnigan and Roger Dollarhide, dedicated jugglers both, for this idea.)

Although this is really the kind of trick that would be perfect if you ever got a job on a desert island or in a lighthouse, you don't absolutely have to. There is an undeniable "Because it's there . . ." sort of appeal to it. Anyone who's read to the last few words of this book is probably at risk of being a five-object juggler.

Good luck.

A **KLUTZ**® Scrapbook

Dear Sir:

I am writing to tell you that your book on juggling works. I was somewhat skeptical at first, not that I doubted your instructions but I was quite aware of my own innate ability.

Now juggling has always interested me and for year wished that I could do it. No~~~~~~~~~~~ ~~t to do this.~~ ~~juggle~~ is not
it was there. Th~~~~~~
as challenging a~~~~~~
to learn to show~~~~~~~~~~~~~~~~~~~~

Your book was f~~~~~~~~~~~~~~~~~~~~~~~~~~~~~~~~~~~
follow. It's fu~~~~~~~~~~~~~~~~~~~~~~~~~~~~~~~~~
such an imposs~~~~~~~~~~~~~~~~~~~~~~~~~~~~~~~
improve my typ~~~~~~~~~~~~~~~~~~~~~~~

They've juggled 3 beanbags into a high-flying business

By BOB LYHNE

Can a person be taken really seriously if he's made it his mission in life to t~~~~~~~~~~~~~~~~~~~

Plaza. We made the beanbags ourselves. We'd sell some, then race home and make some more. We ~~~~~~~ then that we had a multi-million dollar idea.
~~~~~~~ur friend Darrell Hack was just graduating ~~~~~~Stanford Business School and we recruited her ~~~~~from all the big-time bidders like Macy's and ~~~~~National Bank of Boston, and we formed our ~~~~l partnership, Klutz Enterprises."
~~~~~ewhere along in there, Cassidy also enrolled ~~~~ear in the Stanford School of Education, ~~~~as an intern at Mountain View High School, ~~~~ected his credential.
~~~~summer he wrote "Juggling for the Complete ~~~~wherein he asserts that "If you can scramble ~~~~find reverse in a Volkswagen, or stumble ~~~~light switch in the bathroom at night, you ~~~~ how to juggle." Rimbeaux is listed as co-~~~~hat, Cassidy said, is because he gave tech-~~~~stance and also is co-owner of the idea.~~~~ller, a dance student at Stanford, did the

The Founders

The first mimeographed copy – 1977

JUGGLING for the COMPLETE KLUTZ

Dear John,
Thanks for the juggling book. To my suprise I have learned how to juggle already. And I can almost take a bite out of an apple.

Five hands are better than three

By Stewart McBride
Staff correspondent of The Christian Science Monitor
Palo Alto, California
John Cassidy lifts a grapefruit into the air. As it arcs about eye level, he lofts a banana into orbit, shortly followed by a green pippin apple.

ways last chosen when the class picked sides for softball."
Cassidy's aim is to detonate the "juggling mystique that it's all flaming swords. Performers give it all that razzma-tazz but it's much easier than it looks." The book reiterates: "For centuries juggling has been a performer's art. The trick of getting the three objects to dance around your hands has

As Cassidy spreads four dozen red and yellow bea~~ on the table. I gawk at them like the proverbial ki~~ candy store. My lesson begins, straight out of "Jug~~ the Complete Klutz."
Step 1: The Drop. Pick up all three bags and hol~~ briefly. You'll note that there is one more bag than ~~

●e teaches survival in the juggle of life

By Marsha Kay Seff
Staff Writer

ARMED with multiple degrees from Stanford University, John Cassidy started a career with a trio of tennis balls, oranges and soft-boiled eggs.

Meet Mrs. Cassidy's son — the juggler.

The funny thing is that Cassidy isn't much of a juggler. In fact, he's a self-proclaimed klutz. When he's not dropping things, he's boring his audiences by keeping three rather mundane objects dancing around his hands. And that's where his education comes in.

Realizing that graduation would mean an end to his captive audiences, he decided to switch his emphasis from door to teacher. Last year, together with a group of college buddies, he started his own publishing house. Predictably, the first book off the press was a how-to manual on juggling, by the would-be juggler with a bachelor's degree in English and a master's in education.

The best news is that Cassidy ▢ co-author B.C. Rimbeaux's ability ▢ juggle words is far superior to t▢ former act.

▢ble objects. The trouble with oranges is that they tend to roll when dropped; balls tend to bounce, and ▢▢▢ ▢▢ they have a strong tend-

1st edition 1977

2nd edition 1980

3rd edition 1988

4th edition 1994

5th edition 2004

Foreign Editions

More Great Books from Klutz

Potholders

Cats cradle

101 Outrageously Fun Things

Paper Airplanes

Knots

Face Painting

Kids Cooking

Spiral Draw

Star Wars® Folded Flyers

Painted Rocks

Friendship Bracelets

LEGO® Chain Reactions

Can't get enough?

Here are some simple ways to keep the Klutz coming.

1. Order **more of the supplies** that came with this book at klutz.com. It's quick, it's easy and, seriously, where else are you going to find this exact stuff?

2. Get your hands on a copy of **The Klutz Catalog.** To request a free copy, please email **orders@klutz.com**

3. Become a **Klutz Insider** and get e-mail about new releases, special offers, contests, games, goofiness and who-knows-what-all. If you're a grown-up who wants to receive e-mail from Klutz, head to **klutz.com.**

If any of this sounds good to you, but you don't feel like going on-line right now, just give us a call at **1-800-737-4123.**